ARUNDEL

A Picture of the Past

The Mayor of Arundel, 1902-1905:
His Grace the Duke of Norfolk, E.M., K.G.

ARUNDEL

A Picture of the Past

compiled by

JAMES CARTLAND

with help from

T. W. HENDRICK

PHILLIMORE

1978

Published by

PHILLIMORE & CO. LTD.
Shopwyke Hall, Chichester, Sussex

ISBN 0 85033 261 3

Printed in Great Britain by
UNWIN BROTHERS LTD.,
at The Gresham Press, Old Woking, Surrey
and bound by
THE NEWDIGATE PRESS LTD.,
at Book House, Dorking, Surrey

CONTENTS

INTRODUCTION

This book does not attempt to be a history of Arundel—more a record of what has been. In the last 50 years the town has changed radically from being a market-town serving a large country district to a mecca for tourists. Arundel is lucky in that it has escaped the touch of modern progress and still appears to be visually as it was.

As a 'newcomer' I naturally became curious as to the background of my home and I hope that my interest will stimulate other people. Without the help of Tom Hendrick, who has known the town all his working life, this book would never have become a reality.

I would also like to thank all who have helped in any way, especially the following: the Arundel Museum Society; Roger Halls; Mrs. M. Hampshire; Graham Brooks; West Sussex Gazette; H. Mitchell Jacob; Josse Davis; Spencer Swaffer; H. R. Harmer; Chichester Reference Library; Mike Coviello; Charles Rogers; Mr. and Mrs. R. J. Donnelly; W. C. J. Gordon; R. J. Coen; F. Penfold; F. E. Stedman; W. H. Ayling; L. M. B. Davis.

Particularly thanks go to the late 'Skipper' Phillipps, an example of whose writing follows and who spent his life in Arundel. His scrapbook contains much that I have used in this book.

JAMES CARTLAND

'When in action, the performance of this engine was not only effective, it was spectacular. When pumping at high pressure the flames were not confined to the fire which was being dealt with, they sometimes belched vigorously from the chimney of the engine, due to the enthusiasm of the stoker.

Before the fire service was 'nationalised', Arundel possessed two fire brigades —that of the Borough and the private brigade of the Duke of Norfolk. The latter dealt primarily with fires on the Estate, but would also give assistance to the Borough brigade when necessary. As the latter engine was an old 'manual' affair, the attendance of the two brigades was not unusual if the fire was at all serious. The old manual engine was kept inside the Town Hall, from where it had to be manhandled outside, negotiating the two stone steps at the entrance en route.

Meanwhile, someone had gone to fetch the horses. They were supplied by the Norfolk Hotel stables and were usually ready by the time the engine had been winkled out. On summer evenings however, the horses were sometimes turned out to graze in the meadows on the way to the lake. This meant a rush down there to catch the horses, and for this reason, a fire in the winter was preferable for prompt service. But the engine got away eventually and on arrival at the fire, pumping started. A long bar on each side was worked up and down by the fire-men, assisted by anyone else willing to give a hand. Work on the pump qualified for payment so there were plenty of willing volunteers.

The fire alarm system was interesting too. There were two firebells, one on the Town Hall for the Borough brigade, and one behind the 'Victory Inn' in King Street (on the front of a cottage) for the 'Castle' brigade. The first thing a fireman did was to listen carefully, to decide which bell was being rung. That point settled he either made a dash for the engine, (via his home to put on his uniform) or he got on with his work.

Of course we mustn't forget the 'Bridge Wardens'—that was the title given to certain Arundel characters, always hard up, and with no regular employment. They were generally to be found, sitting on a low wall at the approach to the bridge, thereby gaining their title. Some of them looked upon a fire as Manna from Heaven (or beer from a pub). They hurried along after the engine and pumped vigorously.

A friend told me another fire brigade story about a rick fire near the 'Black Rabbit'.

A phone call was received at the Estate Office to the effect that a hayrick had 'got hot inside', and that fire might break out at any time. It was paynight and the Agent asked the assembled men how many firemen were there. Up went several hands and the owners were told 'you had better go and get your tea; there's going to be a fire presently.' Later the bell rang and off they went. On arriving, the heated rick was steaming away more than ever but no fire had yet broken out, so apparently nothing could be done until it did. They couldn't put out a non-existant fire. The suction hose was run out to the river in readiness and for half an hour water was pumped from the river and back to the river again. The engine was a bit temperamental just then, and they didn't want to stop it—it might not like to start again!

All was well, however. The fire duly broke out, was duly put out, and the brigade adjourned to the 'Black Rabbit', where the landlord—to whom the rick belonged—suitably rewarded their efforts; according to one version of the story—too suitably.'

'SKIPPER' PHILLIPPS

THE PLATES

1, 2 & 3. Arundel market had been held in the town since the 13th century. Until the 18th century it was held in 'Old Market Street' (otherwise known as Chepynge Street and from the end of the 18th century as Maltravers Street). Indirectly the change of location can be attributed to the demolition of the old derelict town hall in the 1890s which stood opposite the Norfolk Hotel and to the gift to the town of the well in 1674 by Edward Hamper, the Quaker. This well can be seen in the photographs. By the first war the market had disappeared. These photographs were taken in the 1880s.

ARUNDEL MARKET.

THIS MARKET Opens at 8.30 a.m., and Closes at One o'Clock p.m., by which time all Cattle, Horses, Sheep, and Pigs must be removed.

By Order,

GEORGE LIGHT,

MAYOR.

Arundel,
5th July, 1888.

4. The taxidermist's shop of W. (Benner) Ellis, *c.* 1900. He was kept very busy stuffing the trophies of local sportsmen who, in those pre-conservation days, shot practically everything that moved. Ellis was also a splendid artist. His still life oil paintings are excellent, and his son Ralph was probably the most talented landscape artist born in Arundel. Ralph painted some of the finest inn signs in Sussex. Benner specialised in producing tableaux of small animals similar to those seen in Potter's Museum of Curiosities—owned by the author of this book. When the premises were taken over by Mr. Harry Jacob for use as a stationer's shop (owned by H. Mitchell Jacob for over 40 years) the builder's workmen encountered the corpses of foxes, badgers etc. stored in cupboards by Benner Ellis.

High Street, Arundel

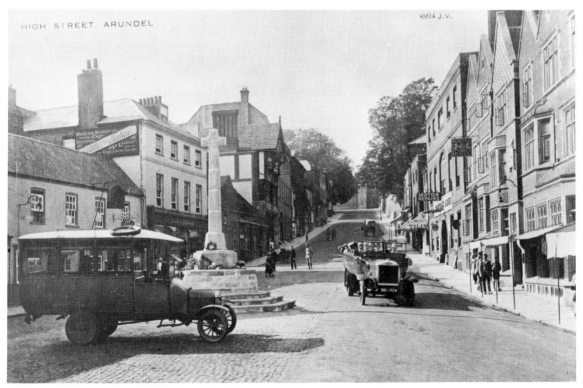

HIGH STREET ARUNDEL

5 & 6. Two views of the market square. The top picture was taken before the advent of the motor car. On the right the London -- Brighton & South Coast Railway delivery van stands outside Pain's, the ironmonger's in about 1898. The bottom picture was taken about 1923. Charabanc tours to Arundel were very popular in the 1920s.

7. This view of Arundel, taken from the corner of Maltravers Street, has changed very little since the beginning of the century, but the war memorial now stands on the site of the old Town Pump, at the bottom of the High Street.

8. Kimpton's 'fancy goods' store and Lucas and Bowen. The latter were well-known for home-made mineral water and ginger beer produced in a factory at the rear of the shop—hence the bottles. The photograph was taken about 1900. The premises were demolished at the beginning of the century and replaced by the half-timbered Lloyds Bank.

9. Interior of Alfred Pain's ironmonger's shop in Arundel High Street, about 1900. This business was taken over by 'Joyce & Pain' in 1869 but Mr. Joyce left after a short time. The old shop was rebuilt in the early 1890s and remains the same today.

10. The Brighton mail about to set off from the Norfolk Arms in Arundel High Street about 1880. The Norfolk Arms was erected by Charles, 10th Duke of Norfolk and apparently cost £7,223 1s. 9d. in 1787. For the first 25 years of its life it was not a great success, as it was used to quarter troops marching to embarkation in Portsmouth. In 1812, for instance, 12,000 soldiers stayed in the hotel—not quite what it was designed for.

11. A somewhat crude artistic impression of the top of Arundel High Street before the erection of the present wall of the castle. 'Dodger' Bartlett not only dealt in malt and hops; he owned the flour mill on the town quay together with the corn warehouse and coal yards. Painted about 1835.

12. Hammond's cycle shop in the market square. This was in a section of the ancient Crown Inn (whose entrance arch can be seen on the right). Taken about 1900.

13. What? No antique shops? Mr. Lapworth, at the turn of the century, surveys the scene with no evident fears of redundancy. Note the baker's hand-cart.

14. Speed fiends! Percy Lapworth, the eminent Arundel printer and stationer propels his aged parent in his motorized velocipede, *c.* 1900.

15.   The Red Lion in Arundel Town Square, *c.* 1910. This was rebuilt in the 1930s--the only surviving part of the old pub being the hanging grapes on the sign today.

16 & 17. Mr. William Woods Mitchell was the founder of the West Sussex Gazette. He was for many years the chief townsman of Arundel, being elected Mayor six times. I think a section from his obituary published in the Hastings & St. Leonards Times in October 1880 shows in what respect his name was held.

'His paper was to be seen in almost every cottage in the district of its wide circulation; and as the power which influences the many should not be despised by the few, the W.S.G. soon found its way into the halls of the country squire and the castles of the nobility. There are wealthy and powerful landlowners in West Sussex, but the greatest among them wielded not the power of the Arundel publisher. And a great many of them seemed to know it. Mr. Mitchell was of much service to his native town. He took great interest in all social questions; was a generous employer of labour; and with his wife and family showed the deepest interest in all engaged in his service.'

The West Sussex Gazette produced its first issue on 1 June, 1853 from its ancient head-office in Arundel High Street. The original printer of the paper was Mr. T. H. Mitchell who had been a general printer for some years. The paper was started with the idea of giving his son William Woods Mitchell a career in which he already had a keen interest. From the beginning the paper was a success and from its first name of Mitchells Monthly Advertiser within a year it was published weekly. Its importance to West Sussex lies in the fact that it was the first paper in and for West Sussex.

18 & 19. The old West Sussex Gazette office. In March 1889 the newspaper contained a graphic description of the fire which gutted its workshops and although the old office fronting the High Street was saved all the machinery was destroyed. By September new machinery was installed and once more the paper was printed from its own premises. In 1899-1900 the old front offices were completely rebuilt in its present mock Tudor style.

20. The annual staff cricket match, in the late 1870s. 6th from the right sitting is Mr. W. W. Mitchell, the founder.

21. Back from the 1st World War, 1918. Outside the High Street Office.

22. Mr. W. Sharp ran his carrying service in the locality and delivered the West Sussex Gazette. He was also the landlord of the 'Victory Inn', Bond Street. The picture was taken about 1895.

23.   Recent investigations by experts have led to the opinion that this is one of a group of Wealden timber-framed buildings erected as early as the 15th century. Situated at the corner of High Street and Maltravers Street (over which it is 'jettied') the premises were used as a butcher's shop or 'shambles'. This building was demolished when the present mock-Tudor houses were built. About 1880.

24.   The left hand buildings designed by Aloysius Hansom (inventor of the Hansom carriage) replaced the Tudor butchers shambles in the 1880s. Sefton House on the right is named after Daniel Sefton, an 18th century lawyer. On the death of his two daughters it passed to the Constable family and was lived in by George Sefton Constable—his godmother was one of the Sefton sisters. About 1905.

25. Arundels first taxi, outside White's Garage in the High Street, about 1910. This business had started as a coach manufacturer's. The coaches were begun at the bottom of the building and finished at the top--then swung out and lowered into the street.

26. Mr. Stedman, the blacksmith outside his foundry off River Road. Behind can be seen Bartlett's Steam Mill. About 1905.

27. In the High Street, Miss Selina Clark's popular sweet shop (*c.* 1920) is on the left of this picture--the premises are now a ladies gown shop. Lasseter's 'Agent for Goss' has hardly changed in over 100 years.

28. Harry Spooner, the shoemaker. This photo was taken when his shop was at Crossbush, near Arundel. Soon after he moved to a shop in the High Street, Arundel. The notice is still hanging outside and much photographed by visitors. About 1905.

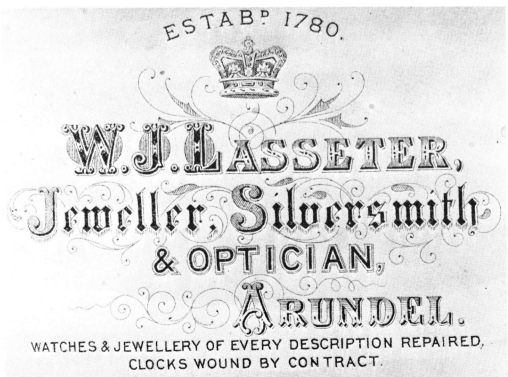

ESTAB? 1780.

W. J. LASSETER,
Jeweller, Silversmith
& OPTICIAN,
ARUNDEL.

WATCHES & JEWELLERY OF EVERY DESCRIPTION REPAIRED,
CLOCKS WOUND BY CONTRACT.

29, 30 & 31. No. 29 shows Mr. W. J. Lasseter, jeweller of High Street, Arundel. His family were clockmakers and jewellers in the town from the end of the 18th century until the 1950s. No. 30 shows the upstairs landing of Mr. Lasseter's shop in about 1910. The shop can be seen in the background of No. 27. No. 31 shows the firm's business card.

32. Ruins of the Maison Dieu which was founded in 1395 by Richard Fitzalan, 14th Earl of Arundel as a hospital refuge for twenty poor men. It originally formed a quadrangle containing a chapel, refectory and chambers for the inmates, who qualified for admission by knowing the Paternoster, Ave Maria and Credo in Latin. The small building in middle background was the boathouse for a small steam yacht, 'Star of the Sea' owned by the Duke of Norfolk in about 1885.

33. Tom Buller's cottage on old Arundel bridge. The Buller family has provided pleasure boats for hire for many generations, right up to the present day. It was reputed that smugglers used this cottage; a trap-door opened in the floor to receive contraband from boats hidden beneath the bridge. The building was demolished in the 1930s.

34. Old Arundel bridge built 1724, demolished 1935. The cantilevered pavements were added in 1831 by the Mayor, William Holmes. Since his personal expenses were not reimbursed he caused the existing admonition to be carved in the stonework—'Be true and just in all your dealings'. The half-timbered block was erected in 1892 to house the new post office. Before this the post office had been in Mr. Broadbridge's shop (now 'Chrisopher's antiques') where a letter could be sent for ½d. normally, or 1d. after 6 o'clock! The picture was taken in about 1904.

35. Lambert and Norris produced gallons of beer at their establishment on Brewery Hill, Tarrant Street— up to the late 1920s. Here is one of their drays; the third horse helped on steep hills. Behind the dray is the 'wattle house' where the market hurdles were stored.

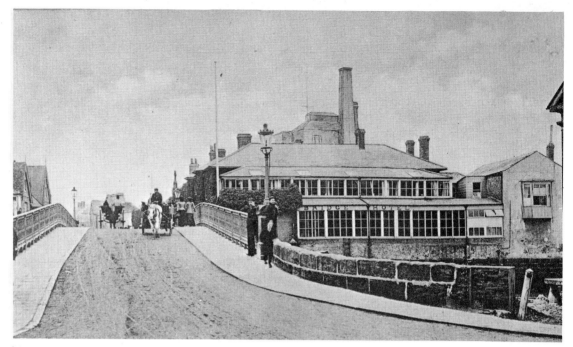

36. Arundel bridge in the early 1900s. The stone fishmonger's table, seen on the right now stands beside the ruins of the Maison Dieu. The hotel collapsed when its foundations were swept away by the river during the rebuilding of the bridge in the 1930s. In the background can be seen the chimney of Constable & Henty's Swallow Brewery, the advertising sign of which, a wooden swallow, is now on the roof of the town hall.

37. The Old Bridge Hotel. This was a typical Georgian coaching inn known at the end of the 18th century as 'The Dolphin'. It was replaced in the 1930s with a less successful building to be seen in the other photographs. On the left hand side can be seen Ivy House, for many years the home of the Constable family who owned the Inn and Constable & Henty's brewery behind. It is said that John Constable, the artist stayed in this house when he visited Arundel in 1834.

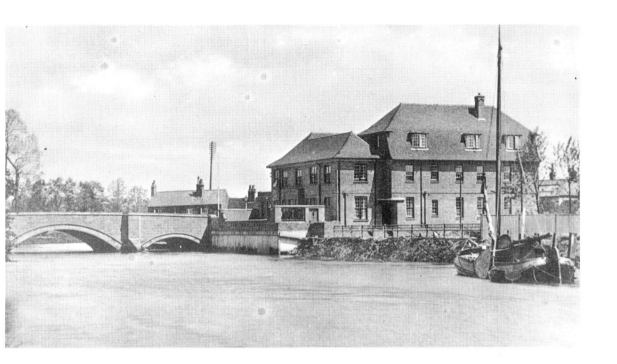

38 & 39. These views of the Bridge Hotel were photographed soon after its opening in the 1930s. It was never intended to replace the gracious old coaching inn that previously stood on this site. Due to an error of judgement, the coffer-dam for the piers of the present dam proved too great a barrier for the waters of the second-fastest flowing river in England; the Arun became diverted under its southern bank and swept away the foundations of the old Bridge Hotel—the building collapsed overnight.

40. The White Hart Inn, King Street. This was demolished in the 1870s and replaced by the present inn and an addition to Mr. Heringtons drapers shop. Although the Herington family had the shop from the 1860s it had been a drapers for at least 50 years before that. Three generations of Heringtons have been Mayors of Arundel.

41. The Swallow Brewery in about 1900. This stood on about the site of the Castle Service Station and was demolished in the 1930s. It was started at the beginning of the 19th century by the Constable family who later in the century went into partnership with the Hentys who owned Henty's bank in the High Street.

42. Arundel, as viewed from the tower of the Swallow Brewery prior to 1892. After that date the new Mill Road passed between both groups of ruins of the Maison Dieu, on its way to Swanbourne Lake and Offham. Note the old shops on the site of the present Post Office.

43.   The corner of Tarrant Street and the High Street. The far building is Watts & Acott, drapers, whose linen department is in the two low buildings. Many of Arundel's prettiest girls worked in the shop, to the delight of local young men! Taken in about 1914.

44.   'Dancing bears were to be seen in the town until about 1914. The small trumpet carried by the owner was to announce their arrival. The bearkeepers used to stay at the 'White Horse Inn', at the top of Brewery Hill, Tarrant Street --4d. ensured a bed and the use of the kitchen. The bear was chained up in the adjoining yard, where the more daring youngsters would open the door to peep inside at the unfortunate beast. The Inn also housed Italian organ-grinders. The 'Blue Hungarian Band' used to visit Arundel twice a week playing outside pubs. Wombwell's Menagerie would pitch in the Square and Sanger's Circus in Daisy Field'. ('Skipper' Phillips)

45.   The Queens Arms Inn, Tarrant Street in about 1895. Although this building still stands it is no longer an inn. It curiously stood next to the Kings Arms which has been there for at least 300 years. The row of cottages with the man outside goes by the name of 'Bung Row' and housed, in the far cottage, the well known local junkman, 'Knocker'Knowles who was known to brandish an ancient sabre at passers-by–it is also the scene of one of Arundel's murders! In the background is 'Sparks furniture depository', founded in 1838—although this building was opened in 1877.

46.   Ancient buildings on the corner of Tarrant Street and Arun Street, taken about 1880. In 1675 Edward Hamper, who had given the town its Market Square well the year before, leased to the Society of Friends (Quakers) at £8 per annum the malt house, stable, mill-house, orchard and garden for use as a meeting-house, and burial ground. On the east side the property adjoined the lower Brew House. Hamper had bought the property from Mary Pellatt, a daughter of John Pellatt of Arundel, later to be Mayor of the town. Hamper was later imprisoned and died in Horsham Gaol for his faith. These buildings were demolished in about 1900. A Tudor doorway can plainly be seen, and the chapel door is on the right of the photograph.

47. 16th century cottages which stood in Tarrant Street opposite the old Co-operative Society shop. They were demolished about 1900. The door with the child in it is the entrance to Charles Ford's boot and shoe shop. The right hand cottage is that of John Burton, cooper by trade, who worked for the Swallow Brewery. The tall Georgian house on the left is the grocer's shop of Mr. and Mrs. Slaughter (the latter nicknamed by the town, Old Nannie Weighfinger) who can be seen in the doorway.

48. The annual Slindon estate workers outing outside 'Mowbray House' Maltravers Street, about 1905.

49.　16th century cottages in Maltravers Street. Demolished in the early 1890s when a new road was cut. The white painted house (3rd from left) was the home of John Tompkins, agent to the Shelley family of Michelgrove. He kept a diary describing life in Arundel at the end of the 18th century. On the left is the building which once housed the Arundel theatre, opened in 1807 by Mr. Thornton and closing within a few years.

50.　Artists and photographers have always considered this to be one of the most picturesque corners of the town. This end of Maltravers Street has remained virtually unchanged since before the beginning of the present century. The left hand cottage used to be the 'Black Bull Inn' in the 17th century and was said to have been mostly knocked down by cannon shot in the Civil War. It still contains a fine 16th century brick fireplace.

51. The Triumphal arch erected for the visit of Queen Victoria and Prince Albert in December 1846. It was put up on about the site of the old Watergate at the lower end of Maltravers Street.

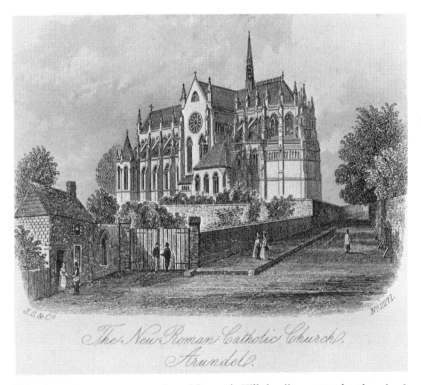

The New Roman Catholic Church.
Arundel.

52. A contemporary engraving of Parson's Hill, leading up to the church of St. Philip Neri—now the Cathedral of Our Lady and St. Philip—c. 1873. The architect for the cathedral was J. A. Hansom—originator of the London Hansom cab.

53. How peaceful was the London Road in the very early years of this century.

54. A riverside view. On the left the present Riverboard stores. The present River Road cuts through the site of the weatherboarded shed on the right, the near part of which is now Hago's. Notice the ladders in the foreground leading to boat moorings. Taken about 1902.

55. (*above*) Diamond Jubilee band, 1897, in Arundel Castle courtyard. The 15th Duke is on the right of the drum.

56. (*right*) God speed to Henry, 15th Duke of Norfolk on his departure to the Boer War in South Africa, in 1900. Looking from the Priory into Maltravers Street.

57.   Lancers drawn up in the square. Probably about 1900 during the Boer War. Arundel was on the main route from London to Portsmouth where the troops embarked.

58.   Welcome home from the Boer War, August 1900. The 15th Duke and his brother, Lord Edmund Talbot, had been away to fight for Queen and Country. Arundel can be seen giving them a joyous welcome. The 'flint' arch is in fact painted wood and was erected specially for the occasion outside the Catholic church (now Arundel Cathedral).

59. The opening of the Arundel drainage works. The 15th Duke of Norfolk (holding the silver trowel) about to lay the foundation stone. On his left is Mayor Roberts and on his right Alderman Alfred Herington. A marvellous collection of Arundel notables can be seen including a lady in a bee-keeping hat(?) and the local policeman. Taken November 4, 1895.

60. The Diamond Jubilee 1897. The Duke declaring the festivities open in Arundel Park.

61 & 62. Celebrations for Queen Victoria's jubilees in 1887 and 1898. The invitation is for the splendid feast laid out in the marquee in the Castle grounds. Everyone is given a commemoration mug—to be seen by each place.

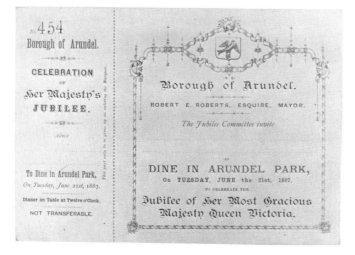

WELCOME HOME 1904

The wedding of Henry, 15th Duke of Norfolk. In 1904 he married the Hon. Gwendolen Constable-Maxwell, daughter of Lord Herries.

63. Arrival at the railway station.

64. Setting off from the station.

65. Welcome from Arundel children.

66. The elders of the town outside the Swallow Brewery.

67. Passing the Mayor and corporation outside the Bridge Hotel.

68. Decorations in the square.

69. Some of the wedding presents in the Barons Hall, Arundel Castle.

70. Henry, 15th Duke of Norfolk in Arundel Park at the annual camp of the 4th Battalion of Royal Sussex Regiment of which he was Colonel. With him are Bernard, Earl of Arundel (later 16th Duke) and Lady Rachel FitzAlan-Howard, taken about 1911.

71. Little Bernard Marmaduke, later to be 16th Duke of Norfolk performs his first public ceremony. He presented colours to the 1st Arundel Boy Scouts. He gave each boy a red silk scarf and a five shilling piece. His father, mother and sisters look on with pride. About 1912.

72. Lady Katherine Fitzalan-Howard and friend, *c.*1915.

73. A Summery scene. The young Earl of Arundel poses between his sisters Lady Katherine and Lady Rachel Fitzalan-Howard, *c.*1914.

74 & 75. Meet of Lord Leconfield's hounds at Hiorne Tower, Arundel Park, 29 December 1913. The 15th Duke was not 'a hunting man' but usually attended this occasion—he can be seen on his horse beside the small child. In the carriage is the 15th Duchess and Bernard, Earl of Arundel (16th Duke).

76 & 77. Two views of the Arundel Regatta, 10 August 1910. This social event continued until about the first World War.

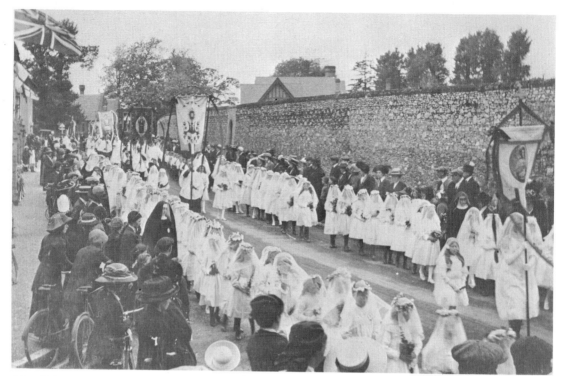

78. Children of Mary walking in the traditional Roman Catholic procession celebrating the Feast of Corpus Christi, in June 1912. To the singing of hymns the Blessed Sacrament is carried over a carpet of flowers in the Cathedral and then, under a canopy, to the quadrangle of Arundel Castle where Benediction is celebrated on an open-air altar.

79. This scene of open-air Benediction in the quadrangle of Arundel Castle took place in the early years of the century, but early in June, to this day, the same feast of Corpus Christi is celebrated in the same way in Arundel by a procession from the Cathedral to the Castle.

80, 81 and 82 (*top overleaf*). Right up to the second World War it was customary for the Volunteers, Yeomanry and units of the Territorials and the Regular Army to hold their summer training camp in Arundel Park. Here are views of the Church Parade--or rather drumhead service--held in front of the Hiorne Tower in 1909 and 1912.

83. There is a notice at each public entrance to Arundel Park warning visitors that whenever a red flag flies, firing is in progress. The range, which runs north along the valley below Pugh Dene is still in use. This picture shows a prize competition in progress for marksmen of F. Company 4th Battalion Royal Sussex Regiment on August 31st 1912.

84. Henry, 15th Duke of Norfolk, performs the opening ceremony at Arundel Lawn Tennis Club. On this sunny day in 1911 Duchess Gwendolen watches the scene with her little son Bernard and daughter Rachel.

85. 'Living Whist'--a colourful diversion for a house-party at Arundel Castle in the early 1900s. The elegant gentlemen at each corner of the lawn were 'dealt' a bevy of 13 beauties each representing a card in the pack. Each lady was 'played' in turn by advancing to the centre--then, each 'trick' of four were led off to the winner's corner.

86. On this occasion in 1911 the Mayor of Arundel Mr. W. Woods Mitchell and his councillors seem to have replaced their cocked hats in favour of rather funereal top hats—an amusing garb for a procession in aid of the local hospital.

87. Bernard Marmaduke, the young Duke of Norfolk in the grand raiment of a Tudor Courtier as he took part in Arundel's Historical Pageant in the early '20s.

88 & 89. The stirring music of a military band was no unusual sound in Arundel before the Great War. Patriotism was in full flower and was an expression of the more positive thinking that then prevailed in England. Here, the Arundelians (or as they are locally called—Mulletts) are viewing with pride one of the parades of its own Royal Sussex Regiment.

THE MAYOR OF ARUNDEL PROCEEDING TO THE MARKET SQUARE
TO PROCLAIM GEORGE V "KING". MAY 9TH 1910.

THREE CHEERS FOR THE KING GEORGE V AFTER THE PROCLAMATION ON MAY 9TH 1910
AT ARUNDEL

90 & 91.   The Mayor and Corporation proclaiming George V King. May 9, 1910.

92 & 93.   In the days before the first World War it was an accepted custom for fit young men to join the 'terriers'--the Territorial Army of spare-time soldiers. These pictures were taken on mobilization the day after the Declaration of War--4 August, 1914. They show that the Arundel Territorials were 'Ready! Aye Ready!'

94. Funeral procession of Henry, 15th Duke of Norfolk, leaving the Catholic church for interment in the FitzAlan chapel, 1917.

95. Unveiling of Arundel war memorial in the town square by Lord Leconfield, 24 July 1921. This replaced the old town pump.

96. Performers in one of the many historical pageants for which the glamorous turrets and ramparts of Arundel Castle have formed such a perfect background. Here, we see victorious Norman horsemen with the somewhat subdued Saxon infantry at the rear. This pageant took place in 1923.

97. Congratulations to Bernard, Duke of Norfolk on attaining his majority. The Mayor and Corporation present the good wishes of the people of Arundel in 1929.

98 & 99. This building, originally a corn store, finally housed a factory for deck chairs. In 1930 the dry timber and canvas caught fire and, despite the efforts of the fire brigades, the building was gutted. It was demolished to form the present Town Quay.

100. On August 29th, 1933 the Mayor, Alderman E. J. Herington, and the Corporation of Arundel proudly presented the Freedom of the Borough to the 1st Battalion of the Royal Sussex Regiment.

101. The people of Arundel welcome Bernard, Duke of Norfolk and his bride, the present Lavinia, Duchess of Norfolk, 20 February 1937.

102. The interior of the Castle keep before restoration in the 1880s and 90s. In the arch on the right can be seen some of the cannon balls fired on the castle in the siege of 1643. Also in the arch can be seen some stuffed owls. These are, or rather were, 'The Keep Owls'. At one time these famous horned owls were said to be the finest in Britain. They were all given names by old Mr. Booker, the keeper at the end of the 18th century, and he is said to have told the Duke that 'Lord Thurlow has laid an egg

103. The grand entrance to Arundel Castle from the quadrangle—prior to reconstruction during the last century. The picture was taken about 1885.

104. The Castle quadrangle was used to store the blocks of stone imported from Caen for the work of restoration *c.*1885-90. This is the same type of stone used by the Norman Earl Montgomery for building the original castle.

105. Rebuilding the Castle in about 1890. Notice the incredible wooden scaffolding and crane, used for hauling stone to the top.

106. Norfolk estate gamekeepers in 1913. Left to right, standing: A. Kinnard, jnr; G. Woodward; Mr. Edmonds; R. Reeves; Mr. Cutler. Seated, left to right: Mr. Northeast; A. Kinnard, snr; G. Osman; C. Campbell; Mr. Hotston; A. Bentley; E. Bentley.

107. Up to the outbreak of the second World War herds of red, fallow and dark Japanese deer roamed Arundel Park—there were even a few Muntjak. The roar of the rutting stags was heard in the late autumn and when the herds were culled, there was venison in the local butchers' shops; stag-horn souvenirs were sold in a shop in the High Street. Descendants of the Arundel deer still lurk in the thickets on the Downs --to the annoyance of the Forestry Commission.

108. 'Yonder Peasant. Who is he?' Gathering winter fuel in the Water Woods.

109. Whiteways Lodge built soon after 1800 by Charles, 32nd Earl of Arundel, at the northern entrance to Arundel Park. The park wall enclosed the old London Road, which the Duke replaced by building the existing road.

110. Bringing in the sheaves, from a cornfield in the Burgesses' Brooks. See how the sheaves were stacked in 'stooks' to aid their drying.

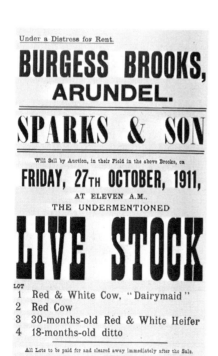

111.

112. Cattle grazing in the water-meadows that now form part of the Wild Fowl Reserve.

113. Mill Road, soon after its opening by its donor, Henry 15th Duke of Norfolk, in 1892. These Lime saplings have grown to form a tunnel of green shade leading to Swanbourne Lake.

114 (*above*),115 & 116 (*overleaf*). Arundel Castle Dairy, built on the site of the old water mill beside Swanbourne Lake. Note how a fountain was provided inside the dairy to keep the atmosphere clean and cool. The style of architecture of the dairy has been repeated in the design of the modern buildings at the adjacent Wild Fowl Reserve. The picture was taken about 1910.

Arundel. The Dairy.

117.   The gratitude of Arundelians and the general public is due to successive generations of Dukes of Norfolk who have permitted free entry to visitors to feast their eyes on this sylvan lake-side scene in Arundel Park. This picture was taken in the middle 1920s.

118.   River trips on motor launches to picnic at the chalk quarries at South Woods are still popular in the summer season.

119.   A view of the cottages forming the 'Black Rabbit' Inn at the turn of the century. From the 1850s it was much frequented by the navvies building the railway and altering the river, and got rather a bad name for fighting and drunkenness. By 1905 it had become one of the sights of Sussex.

120.   Despite the fast sweep of the tide on the bend of the Arun by the 'Black Rabbit', rowing skiffs and gigs were hired out by the 'guvnor', Dan Lee—up till the 1930s—and later, by his successor, Sam Knight.

121.   Looking down from the top of the chalk quarry, the photographer got this birds eye view of the 'Black Rabbit'. Note the chalk barge; the blocks of chalk were used to make good the banks of the Arun. Taken in about 1910.

122.   The women and children of the Harber family, charcoalburners, in Arundel Park by Swanbourne Lake about 1910. This shows a typical charcoalburner's hut—unchanged in design from time immemorial.

123 & 124.   The Old Windmill on Portreeves Acre. This postmill was built about 1769 and was demolished in 1864. It became famous through appearing in John Constable's view of the town. It was replaced by Mr. Atfield's new cement mill in 1861, slightly up-river—which in its turn was destroyed by fire in 1892.

The Windmill Arundel

125. A meet of the Horsham and Crawley foxhounds, on Causeway Hill, February 1908. This scene took place at the now busy junction of the Littlehampton and Worthing roads near Crossbush.

126. House at Park Bottom, Arundel in about 1830, with the pond in the foreground. It is said to have been occupied by relatives of the Duke of Norfolk and he, having no great regard for them, tried to persuade them to give up the tenancy. Failing in this, they were persuaded to take a holiday, to find on their return that the roof of the house had been removed. This happened about the date of the picture.

127. Delivering coal to the gasworks. The Brigantine 'Cleo' (Master W. Steele) was owned like several others by the Robinsons of Littlehampton. On one occasion when being turned for towage to Littlehampton, the 'Ebenezer's' bowsprit knocked down the chimney of a cottage on the opposite bank. Most of the coal for the gasworks came from the north east of England. In 1821, 45 vessels registered as belonging to Arundel. With the coming of the railways the river trade declined, business gradually going to Littlehampton. The final blow came in 1930 when the railway bridge was fixed at Ford. Vessels of 200 tons and more could sail up the river until the 1930s—most ships being towed by the tug 'Jumna'.

128. A barque discharging her cargo of coal at the wharf of the Arundel Co-operative Society.

129.   On the site of an Iron Age defensive ditch, St. Mary's Gate (or Mary Gate) formed the south western entrance through the town wall, erected about 1300. In 1415 a chapel was built by the gate. The gate was demolished by the Parliamentarian General Sir William Waller, when he besieged Arundel in 1643, but was restored to its present condition about 1785 by the Duke of Norfolk and stands in the grounds of the Castle.

130.   The Ford Road in 1909. The lady in the photo was staying at the house marked with an X. This view is almost identical today--even the two shops are still there.

THE PENFOLDS OF ARUNDEL

The Penfolds were originally in business in Arundel High Street where they had what is now Pain's, the ironmongers. They moved to Ford Road and started the Tortington Ironworks about 1870, and they are still there today.

131. The Bungalow, no. 49, Ford Road. Built by James Penfold about 1871 soon after moving his business. Demolished in 1966 to make way for the new fire station.

132. The Penfold family in the garden of 'The Bungalow'. About 1900. Standing, left to right: James Lear; James; Mabel. Sitting, left to right: Percy; Nellie; Mrs. James Penfold (née Fanny Lear); Josephine; Arthur; Reginald Ludgaten (husband of Josephine).

133. Group of workmen at Tortington Iron Works, in front of the blacksmith's shop. They are holding various tools and products of the iron foundry. Taken about 1880.

134. Steam engines, binders, etc. at the works in 1906. Percy Penfold can be seen in the centre front. The men include Drew Johnson, Amos Arnold, Charles Rogers, Ernest Rumsey, Fred Burchell.

135 & 136. Two late 19th century views of the south Marshes windmill built in 1840. It ceased to function in 1919 after storm damage, before this being used for grinding corn by Charles Bartlett, its owner. It still stands, minus its sails.

137.   Until the closure of the swing bridge at Ford Junction in 1932—due to electrification of the Southern Railway—private steam yachts sailed up the river as far as Arundel bridge.

138.   A cargo vessel being towed up-river by the beloved old steam tug 'Jumna'. Up till the 1920s children would run to the river bank when they heard the 'Jumna's' syren. The operations in the busy port of Arundel were a source of continual interest to the townsfolk.